Eliana Hernández-Pachón

The Brush

Translated from the Spanish by Robin Myers

archipelago books

Library of Congress Cataloging-in-Publication Data available upon request.

ISBN: 9781953861863

Poems from *The Brush* appeared in *Firmament*, *Berlin Quarterly*, and *Copper Nickel*.

Archipelago Books
232 3rd Street #A111
Brooklyn, NY 11215
www.archipelagobooks.org

Distributed by Penguin Random House
www.penguinrandomhouse.com

Cover art: Cecilia Vicuña

This work is made possible by the New York State Council on the Arts with the
support of the Office of the Governor and the New York State Legislature.

Obra editada con apoyo del programa Reading Colombia,
cofinanciación a la traducción y publicación.

This publication was made possible with support from the National Endowment for
the Arts, the Hawthornden Foundation, the Nimick Forbesway Foundation, the Carl
Lesnor Family Foundation, Maslow Family Foundation, and Reading Colombia.

Printed in Canada

THE BRUSH

Contents

Pablo

Pablo has
sparse hair on his head
and bags under his eyes like almonds:
he always looks exhausted.

His skin is leather-tough,
his hands clumsy, thickened from working the land,
two marks in the middle of his forehead,
two red furrows form there,
when he's angry, ever since he was a boy,
and now,
when he watches the news at seven,
his eyelids drooping, he says to no one:
this goddamned country
we're doomed this time
and feels a flare of heat in his brow.

His cousins used to tell him
you got the evil eye when you were little.

Pablo has a body like a drum,
a hat is his most prized possession,
when he hugs his friends
he hugs too hard.

Ester lives with Pablo,
lives off the land like him,
tends to their animals,
believes in the evil eye, says it's nothing
but other people's envy,
that's why you shouldn't let babies be seen too much
after they're born.

You also need
to note the time and place:
locate their star
and track it carefully each year.

Ester is patient on the phone:
she spends hours listening
to other people's troubles.

She has a radio from '85 she switches on at lunch,
can kill an animal with a single blow.

Her favorite thing:
eating clementines on the porch.

There's a sweetness in Ester's eyes,
her rounded face,
she knows who people's children are:
when she goes down into the village
everybody tells her their secrets.

Pablo and Ester live up in the hills,
not too far from the ocean.
Their children all moved to the city
and never learned to tend the animals.

Pablo works on Wednesdays and Fridays
peeling tobacco leaves,
walks back through a forest of guayacanes.

Sometimes he gathers strange-shaped rocks
and tucks them in his pocket
with chamomile flowers that Ester likes
and sticks them in a beer bottle once he's home.

They have a Rottweiler,
a cat that mews at the front door:
he misses the kids, says Pablo of the cat and not himself.

Ester gets up early to make coffee,
strains it through a black stocking,
the sun's still hidden.

Some mornings, Pablo finds
dead creatures by the door:
first a hummingbird heavy
as an orange in his hand,
then a snake, a mouse.

Ester watches the creases in the middle of his forehead,
    and says:

the cat's brought you a present,
he's inviting you to hunt:
he's a hunter.

Pablo doesn't believe her, thinks
it's a bad sign, and she insists:
he lives at night, she says,
he lives a different life than ours.

They eat together in the evening, silent,
Pablo's plate between his legs:

one bite for him,
half for the cat.

Pablo carries tobacco leaves
in his arms like ruana cloth.

He also knows exactly when
they can be cut:
they're pale, round-edged,
yellow-veined.

For some time now
he's felt a heavy change pressing the air,
and can't explain it.
Like when
he walks through town at night,
and when he hears the animals
can't sleep.

Meanwhile, the daily tasks loom:
I called you yesterday, he tells his oldest son,
who says a half-asleep hello when he picks up:

what are you doing, why didn't you answer me?

Once a week,
Ester hangs animals
from a metal hook
to drain them of their blood:
there isn't always meat for eating.

She looks at the purple blood on the floor
and thinks
of what the moon brings:
plants underground with the waning crescent,
a yuca harvest with the new.

Somewhere she read: the moon drifts away
3.78 centimeters a year, as fast
as our fingernails grow.
Outside, the neighbors' children play
at seeing who can spit the farthest.

A helicopter roar
wakes Pablo from his nap.

He goes into the yard and sees white papers
tumbling down like snow:

> *EAT YOUR HENS AND SHEEP AND LIVE LIFE*
> *TO THE FULLEST THIS YEAR*
> *BECAUSE THE END IS COMING*

He feels the heat between his eyes.

Best to keep his hands busy,
pace around the house,
shuffle documents.

Fear settles
like a cat in his throat.
Best to crumple them up,
get rid of them outside.

The night before they come
Pablo tosses and turns:
he knows that something's on its way,
can't put his finger on it.

He gets up in the dark,
Ester snores in her fifth dream,
he rummages in the bedside table drawer,
unfurls the fabric that still smells
like wild animal.

In haste, he sees what Ester keeps
in the wooden box:

                        a chain,

                a medallion,

                                some envelopes,

and, finally, the deeds.

                And now who gives a shit.
He grabs the shovel,
takes the shortcut through the fields,

                                        swift,

                then silence.

He switches off the flashlight, thinks
better if no one sees me.

He counts his steps, digs a hole
in the very spot, and does his burying.

He does it when the sky's still dark,
repeats to himself, thirteen

steps, thirteen,
one and three,
not the best number,

best not tell her,
it's always better not to know.

Ester

Standing in the doorway, she tries to think clearly
and looks out to where the woods begin,
snaps her fingers.
     In truth
it was a cloud
shifting in the sky,
and not a sign:
a cloud above them, gray,
with flares of lightning as
a sapphire-hummingbird flitted close

          and I

had better pull some weeds, she says,
stack kindling by the garden, she thinks,
love the dark houses that the hillsides are,
the bones that bear exactly what
the night bears.

But in the woods
it's never really daytime, why
is it so dark, she wonders,
and sinks her hand into the case.
She pulls out the machete and cuts
>her slashing

path: the brush.
She knows
it's dark because the towering trees
won't let the sunlight through.

The insects' swarming zeal,
their great determination,
lets no one sleep out there.
There's wood, it's true, wet wood,
useless for fires.
>There's nowhere she
>can string her hammock up.

Better to keep walking
and if her legs protest
forget her body altogether.

Where could he be, she thinks,
opening her eyes on the first day.
She imagines Pablo
hiding among the leaves,
pictures his body running through the brush
unstitched with pain.

                    No.

He must
have stumbled into something on his way
and gotten bored and started tossing different kinds
of stones into the sky,
becoming, as they fall,
the murmur of the river she can hear.

Crossing the glade, she sees
a shadow vanish
in a glimmer of undergrowth.
Hey! she shouts.
And the woman approaches warily
leading a little girl by the hand.
A whisper first, and now her clearer voice:
They did it to me with a knife, the woman says
and points to a mark on her arm.
They also did things
I can't talk about.

They walk by day. The little girl
doesn't like talking much.
At night, they search the sky for the Southern Cross,
but no one sleeps much anyway.

In the brush
there's no time for sadness, she thinks
with sleep-injected eyes,
palms damp,
lines striping them red.

The little girl needs a place to rest.

And like a sudden downpour
come the questions, like
could it have been what I just heard please no?
should I have waited for him there?

The brush forgets the animals,
the rain falls harder, swallowing
the questions.

Ester imagines
the weeds creeping into the house,
thinks of everything
left unfinished.

They can hear voices from the brush,
the moss films over the most silvered stones.
It was nothing, she sighs.
Then she tramples two snails:
damned drizzle again.
She asks: was it a bad sign
that the cat never came back?
What happens when a forest animal
looks right into your eyes:
the teeth that are its eyes,
the madness

                nesting there
after so many days in the woods.
Best not to think at all. Best
to list the things she likes to do:
scatter corn for the chickens
trim the garden
sink her hands
into the fresh
milk for cheese.

I want to tell you,
the woman says one night,
what happened that day,
like if the power had gone out,
if the fan was rattling.
I don't remember the noise,
I only remember
the fan in the bedroom
shaking its head
no no no
and then when we tried to leave
the Sunday bus never came.

She sees rotten fruit on the ground,
guavas that can't be eaten,
seething with ants.
At night she wonders:
what was my sin?
what was my mistake?
is the brush a man or a woman?

She forgot she'd said:
no more questions
to stem the hate.
And yet she hears
the woman screaming in her sleep,
can't help but wonder
what it feels like if your body shuts off
and your heart, an engine, won't start again.
The forest throbs inside,
and outside are the ants, the cachitos,
and she forgets the menace for a moment.

She wishes she could leave,
could push away
the branches of the wild thickets in the air,
and say at any moment:
I don't even think of hunger anymore.
But then it's dusk again,
the moon accompanied
by tiny white flecks in the water.
At night, they forget again, the current swells.
Where did you find that shirt?
I wrung it out yesterday, the little girl responds,
I pulled it from the river with a stick.

The Brush

The limbs crisscrossing deep inside the woods
are numberless. They have a vital purpose,
like stout fingers passed down by blood,
and everything that falls
inexorably from the sky:
torrential rain.

Rainwater batters scabs,
rainwater pummels the sturdy legs,
rainwater wets things with its tongue,
the tiny buds, the swamps,
the green course of the littoral.

And so
the thistles part like frailejones,
the gentians, acacias, and periwinkles,
the wild geraniums,
the folding orchids and the plegaderas
that only grow far from the sea,

and in that tangled grove
that struggles to digest the land
are thickets in ravines now hidden to the eye.
The forest's hair snags angrily. They snap
and snap, the hanging beards of lichen.

The Investigators explain:

Seventy more of those bullets are fired that day. A mere ten strike the trees. As the bullets are fired, cheerful music plays. Cheerful music plays because, having fired the bullets, they want to play the drums. Before gathering everyone in the town square to ask the mandatory questions, they bring out the audio equipment and drums from the houses and play this cheerful music loud and clear. In everyone's ears, the clamor of the bullets muddles with the drumroll.

The Witnesses say:

Yes, we heard something, but we said nothing, we couldn't say anything, the rainwater swarmed on the windowsills. We heard something, but it was a snail-trail slicking along, the summer heat, irritation licking our faces: we thought it was the click-clack of the train. We said nothing, and anyway, what could we have said that they would've heard, didn't everyone know by then? We're real men. If we open our mouths, will we be able to forget?

We left.

Northward from the forest, as we know, blows the wind, generous.

The Brush returns:

Everything green
that grows
torrential slips along,
caresses cachitos and bromelias,
peels back their emeraldness.
And from that dense
green snarl
there comes the scrape of limbs colliding in the air,
the thickets tearing at a clayey soil.
Heard from the open sky,
the branches creak,
and then
a foot thrust in the air:
a raised leg takes a step.

The Brush continues:

When the bodies collapse in the town square,
picked out at random,
the houses are left behind with their yards,
their kitchens, their sheets pressed smooth,
receiving, still,
the sun's warm touch.
Things are left with their layers
creased into each other,
asking why,
this,
now,
things don't think before speaking,
they charge ahead
like old trains
derailing.

The Investigators ask:

What did they do to them? Did they kill the ones they killed because they were on the list, or because they tried to defend themselves? What else did they do that day? Was there any warning? How did they get here? That other boy—why did they take him away? Who said he'd stolen their animals? We heard about the man riding a burro. Where did that happen? How did that happen? How many did they shatter into? Were the connections made a long time ago, or were they made and unmade again and again? Did they stay behind as lookouts? Did they leave? Did they leave after that day?

The Witnesses say:

That day, when they reached the village, they asked if guerrillas lived there, if they had women there, if they danced. Also if the women cooked for them there, if the sun beat down hard there, if they took the occasional stroll. As they asked, they wanted to know if they'd gone to the end of the world, if they'd made love there, if they had roosters and if their roosters sang or crowed. If they sang with the sun, like normal roosters, or if they were confused and sang at eleven, at seven, at ten o'clock. If there were days when they didn't sing at all.

The Investigators announce:

From the intersection, you advance twelve meters east along the road. The same distance can be measured in trees or in fourteen of a young man's paces. The entrance to the house is located beside a wall, five meters from that point on the road, on the northern side. We found scraps of pamphlets around the perimeter; once pieced back together, they read:

> *EAT THE HENS AND SHEEP*
> *AND LIVE LIFE TO THE FULLEST*

We have indicated another point on the map: 342 meters from the house, three degrees north of the intersection, someone had dug a hole. There was a box inside.

The Brush says:

Their bones,
their last palpable forms,
distill into erasure what
they used to be:
masses, birthmarks,
then soil and humus, simple tissue
that the weight of passing days
slowly compacts into
a coat of gauzy earth.

The Investigators explain:

There are, however, no surviving photographs of that day. There is one from the day before, located in an envelope, in the wooden box that was found in the woods. In the background, to the left, a man in a hat is wondering where to put things. Also in the background, to the right, hard to discern in the overexposed image, they are laying out a little boy in the sun. Given the women's attire, and because the found body had two lines on the forehead, we can infer that the boy was him: Pablo Rodríguez.

His wife, Ester Martínez, in an official ID photo, looks directly into the camera.

Witnesses state that she often said, following the event, "I haven't liked the taste of food ever since I came back from the woods."

The Investigators point out:

The bullet traced a parabolic path that may be described as follows: a line is born from a man's outstretched hand and forms a curve, rises to its zenith, and then contracts, arcs downward, can be heard among other bullets: *tra-ca-ta-ca-TA*. The air's resistance slows its flight. Even so, the bullet entered through the right side.

Witnesses state that women in rocking chairs had complained about the weather, remarking on the stillness of the air.

The Brush says:

Beneath the sun's great squall,
charred black insects rest,
and children bury ducks so that they'll sprout and grow:
the leaves are newly dry,
the buds,
their coloring decayed.

It's common knowledge that if salt should burgeon
from the ground and form
two sandy hollows,
two stones
should mark the way.
But if nobody knows how to contain the salt
or make it bloom again inside the graves,
the facts will crystallize
like an irruption, accidental,
extraordinary,
and not the detonation
of a long-brewed plan.

When the moment came, it felt like a wasp
boring into the spine from within,
then the flash,
then nothing.

The Brush clarifies:

If matter is human,
this brush, which breathes,
follows the current of itself,
and is a substance that decays
and eats itself
and comes back into being:
breathing, furious.
Everything envelops it:
larvae, their patience,
naked mushrooms, the hypnotic
scent of flowers.
During the concert,
rain is generality.
Every *I* and every *mine*
is open sky or moss.
It loses its possessive, but
it's water pooling densely,
breeding tadpoles.

The Witnesses resume:

If we add the fact that the night entered the houses with them, the night came and went as it pleased, extending its dark sky as skin is stretched, as God covered the body of the animals with hides, if we may borrow the image, which is to say, enveloping it all, if you add the fact of the night in all its vastness and envelopment, you might come up with an idea.

The Brush remarks:

Before the night's expanse,
life's hidden forms:
the stubborn ferns and dogwood,
the ruthless concert of cicadas,
the seed of honey:
how could you not be proud,
not join that inflorescence,
indestructible and ravishing?
Meanwhile, the rain intensifies,
and interrupts the sleep of children in their beds,
adjourns the daylight with its sentence.

The Investigators point out:

Subsequently, the men checked all their hands and shoulders, searching for marks that might betray having carried tents, having touched weapons, having brushed against the woods as evidence. They searched for signs, like the absence of hair on the calves due to the constant use of boots, like blisters on the feet from walking. They fenced them in around the hills, and blinded by the boiling blood, they charged—it must be emphasized—at them, supported by no evidence at all.

The Investigators continue:

They reach the town like a triumphal march, an astonishing entrance: the exhibition of an omnipotence that could be called defiant at the very least. Even so, we were unable to determine the number of women who were forced to cook, of men and women who were forced to watch, of women and children who were locked up. It is necessary to establish the number of people whose property was damaged, whether fire was used to destroy said property. It is imperative to elucidate the circumstances of the means, time, and place. Still others cannot be understood: why a ghost plane flew overhead in the dead of night, how was it that the authorities heard, and why, when they heard, they failed to lend their ears for a moment, what they were doing, we don't know, and why they arrived when there was no longer anything to be done.

The Witnesses correct:

More than a march, it came with all the force of a stampede, the late arrival of a storm absorbing all the air into its sultriness. They wanted everything. A muddle, everything: they wanted some to talk but only say what they wanted to hear, they wanted all the animals to make no noise, they wanted to sing but hear the music all at once. They wanted everyone to take it like a man. They had to have exactly what they wanted, as they wanted it, they were like spoiled children, wanting everyone to watch, to listen, to know, they wanted to be heard everywhere. They wanted to display themselves in front of everyone as the night displays itself, everyone helpless to do anything about it.

The Witnesses add:

We heard about the first and said, optimistically: there must be a reason, he must have done something, he was probably up to no good, anyone sneaking around the honey pot will get something stuck to him.

Then we learned it was a relative, Don Pablo, who'd gone out to the road to pick some corn.

When what happened happened and they made us watch, it was as if the Earth revolved around our eyes, as if space opened up between our eyes, as if a lava flow erupted from within. *Come out, you savages. All of you are going to die today*, they said.

We tried to bar the doors.

Some had fled into the brush by then.

The Brush says:

After the confusion and the night
a light flares from the houses,
deeper in, a light so strong
it swallows up the night:
a group, a throng of joy,
has disobeyed the order of the night,
accompanied, in their stubbornness to live,
by the desiring flowers, plants
and their pulsing nocturnal breath.
Together, infringing on the threat
of night, the stark command against their gathering,
they're earthbound stars beyond the night,
a long-lifed swarm, so many of them,
and just one night.

The Brush continues:

The questions still survive:
what does it think about, the brush, somnambulist,
after it's seen it all?
The day that follows night returns
its artifice, the well-known
interlocking of the hours:
how is it that time didn't stop,
why do the grain's unopened eyes
keep growing?
After the night
day breaks again like a correction
or a punishment:
the leaves wake warm out of the dark
and liven with the dew
and the voice of the brush, its creatures' din,
is still a concert,
merciless and shrill,
and yet a concert all the same.
It's always moving forward:
there isn't time to stop inventing things,
and in its first honey, still hot,
the names accumulate.

The Investigators detail:

It has become impossible not to acknowledge what was hidden; namely, a clue: the box. Inside it, the abovementioned photographs, a chain of negligible value, and, more importantly, some deeds, evidence that there was no crime, no motive, no surprise for us. The deeds certify Pablo Rodríguez, leader of the Community Action Council, legal owner of the property, who, before his capture and murder in the town square, buried his belongings. What remains incomprehensible is how so many people taking so many different routes, is how no one can be detected, combatted, or captured, the incredible part is that nothing affected their thinking, more surprising still is the fact that no one knows anything, nothing, nothing ever responds.

The Brush says:

As time goes on, the women,
defying the night's threat,
traverse the brush, their skin awake,
keep clamoring despite the night,
united into a persistent stream.
Little by little, their daily tasks
· become the heart of day again:
peeling, eating, washing,
verbs attached to concrete objects:
knife, dish, herbs,
the spade that spreads their shadow will come later.
It's them, not flowers,
an inflorescence all together,
radiant as fireflies,
the love that rises from them like coral reef.
Invincible, a stone clutched in each hand,
more in their pockets,
mens' questions disregarded,
their prohibitions mocked:
don't go out after seven,

don't gather as a group for any reason.
The brush climbs up into the trees,
another blaze
amid the shifting of their steps.
And what if there was something taller than the night,
higher up, riddling the sky with holes?
They hear the nearby clouds
arranging thunderclaps, still dense and fierce,
a warm hum in the jungle.
Below, their pounding hearts:
their red manes listen,
facing the wind.

The Brush adds:

For those who came back:
a handful of totumo blossoms,
piñuelas with their tender pulp,
their starry white tomentum.
These fleshy-petaled flowers,
vanilla-fragrant in the night,
and other flowers, furious,
experts in disobedience:
the many-flowered heliconia,
the hidden thorns that snag the skin.
An invasion of bougainvillea,
a parade crowned by tireless sepals.
Some, the ones with calyxes, accompany the fruit,
others are sterile; clusters, too,
of yellow cestrum flowers,
of candelabra flowers,
and of the flower they call amor que zumba,
love abuzz—
abundant clusters,
blooming from themselves.

Between February 16 and 21, 2000, members of the Autodefensas Unidas de Colombia (AUC, United Self-Defense Forces of Colombia), commanded by alias "Jorge 40" and alias "Cadena," killed sixty people in the Montes de María region. During this incident, known as the Massacre of El Salado, paramilitary forces tortured, slashed, decapitated, and sexually assaulted the defenseless population, forcing their relatives and neighbors to watch the executions. Throughout, the militiamen played drums they found in the village cultural center and blasted music on speakers they took from people's homes.

The several-day massacre prompted the mass evacuation of the inhabitants of El Salado and neighboring villages. Many were killed as they attempted to flee. The paramilitary forces faced no opposition: one day prior, the Colombian Marine Corps battalion that was responsible for protecting the area had withdrawn. The Massacre of El Salado is one of forty-two mass murders carried out between 1999 and 2001, leaving a total of 354 victims in this region.

Two years later, and in spite of state obstruction, many inhabitants of El Salado and nearby villages returned. Some went on to found community organizations like Mujeres Unidas de El Salado (United Women of El Salado).

On July 8, 2011—eleven years later—the then-president of Colombia apologized to the community for the absence of public forces during the events. In 2012, the residents of El Salado agreed to join the collective reparations program of the Comisión Nacional de Reparación y Reconciliación (CNRR, National Commission for Reparations and Reconciliation).

This book is based on the report about the massacre that was released in 2009 by the Centro Nacional de Memoria Histórica (National Center of Historical Memory). The names and stories included here, though drawn from real events, are fictional. The excerpts taken from the report are capitalized and italicized in *The Brush*.

How to Narrate Horror?

There are many ways to narrate horror, and it's hard to know which one is right. A dry, detached notarial record full of specific data and times, numbers, measurements, like a forensic report? A journalistic chronicle, be it objective or subjective, that tries to access the suffering of the victims? A fantastical reenactment in which terror swells unnoticed? A devastating, symbol-laden poem in the style of Paul Celan? A fictionless novel in the vein of Primo Levi or Truman Capote?

The Brush, by Eliana Hernández-Pachón, recounts one of the worst massacres in early twentieth century Colombia, committed by paramilitary forces (with obvious military complicity) in the village of El Salado and its environs, the Montes de María. Here, the author chooses a seemingly straightforward way to narrate horror: narrative poetry in third person that describes what befalls a peasant couple (two indirect voices, Pablo and Ester) as soon as signs suggest that something terrible is about to happen. The language is serene, colloquial, familiar, and the voices issue from the mouths of these names: Pablo, Ester, Pablo, Ester, husband and wife. The omens, the fear, the warnings flutter down like snow from the sky. When the threats of danger intensify, Pablo decides to bury his sole treasure, a small box, in a secret place: in case he survives, or in case someone from his family survives.

The account unfurls slowly, slantwise, in a way that feels barely insinuated, subtle, never explicit. The language is simple, accessible, yet oblique, as if shrouded in mist at dawn, or hidden in the shadows of the brush, the undergrowth, the tropical thickets that tangle and obstruct our sight; granting only partial glimpses, only letting in the light, the truth, through machete blows clearing a path. Signs, suggestions, uncertain portents. And the reaction to fear: best not to think at all. Or to think of pleasant things.

The book doesn't spurn the fantastical. Humans aren't the only beings who speak. Animals, too, send out their signals, and the brush, the forest, communicates; it whispers, describes, imparts. The brush may be the main character in this story. But when the narrative grows unreal, almost dreamlike, the prose of the world bursts in, the language of forensic reports. The Investigators speak in prose, copying what the Witnesses say. When it comes to reconstructing horror, there is invariably a moment when prose— Cartesian reason—invades.

The Witnesses have more poetry in their account than the Investigators do. It's best to speak obliquely of horror, especially for those who have suffered it firsthand. Poetry grants them an indisputable dignity, a sense of honor beyond the scream of panic, the literal repetition of the massacre in blood-soaked words. Perhaps that's why the Brush speaks too: trees, weeds, ferns, and wildflowers are all witnesses to what occurred. The Investigators seek to restore to the Witnesses—and to the Brush, if possible—the explicit language of reason: lists, motives, numbers, data, accusations explaining why one person was killed and another was not. Why were the villagers forced to watch the massacre? Why did the killers play festive music while they did their killing? How long did it take, who did it, in what order, with whose help? The poet, steady-handed, resists this prosaic impulse.

The Investigators study, measure, use cardinal directions, delve deeper, even discover the treasure hidden before the massacre; it may not be worth much, but it's what belonged to Pablo, one of the victims, one of the sixty people murdered in the Massacre at El Salado. The Brush, for its part, only speaks of how the bones start to decompose underground, how human beings slowly turn to humus, the jungle's mulch. The two languages confront or complement each other. The aloof account and its data; the images of those who saw, and who understand more deeply through metaphors than through stark, raw facts that simply replicate the atrocities.

Ultimately, The Brush, the natural world serenely speaking its piece, is the only all-knowing, all-understanding presence here—and perhaps what can set things in motion again, in favor of life and against death. The result is a moving one, and it grants the victims all the dignity they had and still have.

Héctor Abad